A SALES GURU'S SECRET

A SALES GURU'S SECRET

HOW TO BECOME A MASTER OF SELLING

Yassini A. Kapuya

**TBX- Business Consulting Co.
Stanford, California.**

ISBN 978-1514225974

Published by TBX- Business Consulting Co.
P.O. BOX 19604 Stanford, CA 94309
www.tbxconsulting.com

First edition, June 2015.

Edited by Catherine Weaver

Designed by Sigillum Publishers
www.sigillumpublishers.com

Printed in the United States of America

ACKNOWLEDGEMENTS

By the grace of God, I'd like to give special thanks to the Lord, who has given me enough understanding and willpower to write books, as this is my third book, "A Sales Guru's Secret". Also, I'd like to give my sincere appreciation to my parents Anthumani and Tausi Kapuya, who taught me the philosophy of wisdom which has helped me shape my life, and who helped me realize that if I need a change in my life it has to come from me, and that I shouldn't complain about what I don't have but work with what I have, to improve myself and others whenever I can.

I would also like to give special thanks to Mr. Katankola, who gave me my first job as a book salesperson in Kaliua, Tabora in Tanzania. My thanks also go to my Mlimani Primary School teacher in Dar-es-salaam, Mrs. Grace Elia, who endorsed me as chairperson in the sales committee at standard 7; a Wells Fargo Bank Manager in Mountain View, California, Miss Reena S. Carvallo, who encouraged me and believed in my ability to succeed in selling bank products; and my son Amani Kapuya for listening and giving me his feedback about the topics and issues in most of my books.

You can order all books on line at: www.amazon.com and at different book stores. Also, you can order direct from us at: tbxconsulting@yahoo.com

Follow us on Facebook and Twitter

INTRODUCTION

In this book you are going to learn the five pillars of how to become a master of selling. In general to be successful in the art of sales, based on my personal experience and what I have seen from others, the key is that you must like selling and have good communication skills, because you will be constantly in contact with people where you have to define and explain what you're offering them. The five pillars to master the art of sales are:

- You must love to sell.
- You must be willing to learn the customer's behavior in the market you want to serve.
- You must be up-to-date with shopping trends, because with time shopping methods change, and so methods and techniques of selling change.
- If you are selling products, you must learn and understand your products well so you can explain to the customer how the products work; this will instill customer confidence in you.
- In service, since you are mostly selling something that is invisible, your credibility and sincerity must be high, because if people trust you then they will do business with you.

Therefore, I have no doubt in my mind that you will find a lot of points which will help you to realize and open up new opportunities in your life as you become a salesperson and start making money. These five pillars have worked for others, and for me at Wells Fargo Bank and in my own business for over 30 years. I believe they will work for you too, and you will be able to sell well (as long as you are willing to apply yourself) and then you will be among the top sales gurus.

TABLE OF CONTENTS

CHAPTER ONE

SALES

❧ THE EXPECTED LESSONS IN CHAPTER ONE ☙

What is a sale?

Why do you choose a sales career?

Why is your ability to communicate very crucial?

What are the 21 characteristics of a sales guru?

My personal sales experience.

"Pretend that every single person you meet has a sign around his or her neck that says, 'Make me feel important.' Not only will you succeed in sales, you will succeed in life." —Mary Kay Ash

WHAT IS A SALE?

Salesmanship is an art which either comes naturally, is learned in school or is self-taught as life goes on. In general, we are all salespeople; we have to sell products, services or ideas to be able to earn money or to let the public know the benefit of what we have to offer to the society. Thus the art of selling is very crucial in our lives. The key is that if you can communicate well with your customers, most of the time you will succeed, and by doing so you have mastered one of the pillars of selling. Sales is an exchange of goods and services at added value, so your ability to communicate with the customers, whom you are trying to convince that what you are trying to sell has a benefit to their livelihood, will separate you from the rest of the salespeople in your group.

WHY DO YOU LOVE SELLING?

A sales job is like any other career in life. Some of the sales gurus' secrets which make them the best in selling are that they love helping people, they are hungry to save people money, and they love providing customers with good quality products or services; which are good-sounding promises for improving and satisfying customers' quality of life. Always remember in any career you choose to pursue, to first keep in mind serving people before thinking about making a sale or money. This will help you create the human relationship which is key to your success in life, and especially in sales. Don't just say, "I love sales so I can make more money." That is a wrong reason to go into sales: just to make money.

THE CHARACTERISTICS OF A SALESPERSON

No one can define the characteristics of a salesperson. There is no specific characteristic that indicates that this one is a sales-type person or that one is not; we are all salespeople, as we are constantly selling something to somebody every day. The difference is what you are selling and to whom, and that will tell you where you fit in sales.

You may be good at selling products, services, or ideas. Thus it's up to you to see what you are best at, or that you like selling the most. For example, politicians are good at selling their ideas about how they think the society is going to benefit, business consultants and motivational speakers are good at selling their personal experience and history to empower individuals so they don't make unnecessary mistakes in the process of trying to achieve their goals, and merchants are good at selling goods. Thus, look at what fits you the most and what you love doing, and that will be your driving force in bettering your career in sales.

THE 21 CHARACTARISTICS OF TOP SALES GURUS

IF YOUR ANSWER 'YES' TO ALL THE BELOW, THEN YOU ARE ON YOUR WAY TO BECOMING A MASTER OF SELLING.

1. They are very friendly people.
In sales you are trying to build a relationship with your customers before you even close a sale, and your friendly attitude will create a warm welcome and get your customers engaged. This makes it easier to sell your products to anyone.

Yes ☐   No ☐

Why --
----

2. They are very approachable as individuals.
People like to work with or talk to someone whom they feel comfortable with and who are not stuck up. Be open and loose, let your face and smile say, "Come and let's work together to solve your problem."

Yes ☐   No ☐

Why --
----

3. They can control their anger anytime.
In sales you meet people with different feelings, opinions and emotional states, so if you can't control your anger it's hard for you to even make them calm down and to sell the products to them.

Yes ☐   No ☐

Why --
----

4. They are not egotistical people.
The biggest barrier between you and customers is your ego; the people you look down on are the ones most likely to buy more from you. Be a people-person and love each and every one equally. You never know who could be your potential customer.

Yes ☐   No ☐

Why --
----

5. They show concern about other people (empathy).
Your sales will go up because of your empathy toward other people's needs

and wants. This will show that what you are selling is something good, durable and useful to them, just as if it were for yourself.

Yes ☐   No ☐

Why --
----

6. They are problem solvers.
When people come to buy something they are looking for a solution, so you must be aware of how what you're selling could be of benefit to the customer, so you can demonstrate and make them say, "Wow, this is what I was looking for!" Then you will make a sale. Don't let the customer have a doubt about how the products you explain to them are going to solve their problem.

Yes ☐   No ☐

Why --
----

7. They are good listeners.
You must be good at listening to the customers; otherwise you will not understand what their needs and wants are. If you understand what they need you don't have to keep asking them questions. When you keep asking questions it can create doubt in your customers about whether you really know what you are selling or not.

Yes ☐   No ☐

Why --

---

8. They have a natural and sincere smile.
People can tell the difference between a fake and a natural smile. Most salespeople have very genuine smiles that make the customer smile with them, and this creates a very conducive environment and opens the way to more questions and discussions which lead to closing the sale.

Yes ☐   No ☐

Why --
----

9. They have the ability to conquer fear.
In sales you are going to meet lots of challenges: sometimes people are selling the same thing in the same street or town, with a better location or more experience. But if you conquer your fear, you will sell with your head up and not be intimidated, because everyone starts from somewhere until they rise up, so just go and do it. Success comes with hard work and experience.

Yes ☐   No ☐

Why --
----

10. They are not judgmental people.
There is a saying: "Don't judge a book by its cover." So treat each and every person as a potential customer. Some may come in the form of testing you to see whether you're really there to help them solve their problem before they buy a product, or if you're just there to make money and you don't care about fulfilling their needs.

Yes ☐   No ☐

Why --

11. They don't assume things.
Don't assume things. Be specific, and your specification will build confidence in your customers that what they're buying will work and suit their needs. Just remember – if you are not sure yourself about what you are selling, do you think your customers are going to believe in you? In this case you may lose a sale.

Yes ☐   No ☐

Why _____
_____

12. They are full of energy and excited with their work.
In sales sometimes, or most of the time, customers come to seek a solution. Your energy and excitement will boost their morale and get them into the mood of buying. This can begin a conversation about the products, and sometimes you can use the excitement to convince the customer to buy them.

Yes ☐   No ☐

Why _____
_____

13. They have positive thinking and a creative mind.
Your positive thinking and creative mind will help you boost your morale. Even if sales are down, you can try different methods and tactics. In most cases in sales, different customers have different approaches, and your creative thinking will help you be alert and know what your next move for different customers would be when sales are slow. If it's not working for one customer, it may work for the other one; the key is not to give up or beat yourself up because so-and-so didn't buy, or sales are slow – just be creative.

Yes ☐   No ☐

Why --
----

14. They have a good memory.
Try to remember the name and the favorite thing of your customers; this will create true friendships and you can sell them what they need. People always like to go where they are known. For example, if the customer walks in and you say, "Hi, Mr. (or Mrs. or Miss) So-and-So," they feel important and that their business is appreciated by you. In return they will tell their family and friends that you treat them well, and they will recommend you to other customers because you care about their wellbeing.

Yes ☐   No ☐

Why --
----

15. They dress for success to reflect their image.
People like to work with someone who looks good. This makes you look less intimidating to them and it can tell a lot about your character, especially in the sales force. Before someone talks to you they look at how you present yourself in society, so try to look good; this will attract potential buyers to what you're offering.

Yes ☐   No ☐

Why --
----

16. They are open-minded to new ideas.
As a salesperson and also as a normal human being, you don't know everything. Thus to succeed in sales, learn from others; try new methods of approaching your potential customers, and be willing to receive con-

structive criticism; this will also be a learning opportunity for you to do better not only in life, but in sales.

Yes ☐   No ☐

Why --
----

17. They are good communicators.
Communication skills are very crucial in life as well as in sales. If you can communicate well you will be able to persuade the buyer that what you are offering them adds value to their life. Usually customers look for solutions to their problems and your job is to define and explain the product as a solution to their problem.

Yes ☐   No ☐

Why --
----

18. They are eager to learn
Learning is a lifelong process – there is no limit to knowledge. The more knowledgeable you are about the industry you are selling in, the better equipped you are to answer the many questions that may arise from your customers during a sale. In other words, more knowledge helps you think outside the box and sell well.

Yes ☐   No ☐

Why --
----

19. They are passionate in their work, not only for the money, but also to help people.

You must ask yourself why you want to be a salesperson. Is it for love, making money, or helping people solve their problems? Your choice will determine the direction of either your success or failure in sales. Most sales gurus don't just sell to make money, but they love what they do and that motivates them to work hard and help solve other people's problems. That requires passion and a desire that comes from within to help people, and that is your driving force to sales success.

Yes ☐   No ☐

Why _____
_____

20. They love to sell.

If you love something you will learn or work hard until you get it. For example, the first three months at Wells Fargo Bank were hard for me; I didn't know anything about the banking industry and its products, but I loved to sell. So I studied very hard until I became one of the banking sales consultants.

This tells you that you may not be good in sales at the beginning, but don't let that stop you because love will force you to work hard to learn until you become a master. Some are natural-born in sales but some learn to become salespeople. All these business schools teach people how to sell, but in most cases people who are taught already love to sell, but they just want to know how to sell well. There is a saying, "You can drag a horse to water but you can't make it drink." If someone doesn't like to sell, no matter how many PhDs in sales they have, they will not make it to the top.

Yes ☐   No ☐

Why _____
_____

21. They possess good ethics and moral standards.

People like to be treated with respect and integrity, and as a salesperson you must hold a high ethical and moral standard. Then you will see other people's feelings and you will help them with respect. If you are ethical then you will keep your word, and you will serve customers with no bias, and this will create more customers because they will feel you make them as important as anyone in their own life.

Yes ☐   No ☐

Why --

APPLICATION

Find out and see where you fit or you do well, and use that as a sales base to enhance your passion. For example, if you like to sell products, then open a store or work in the retail industry, if you like to sell your ideas, thinking that you can improve society, then you may consider being a politician, and if you like to sell services which empower the individual, then be a business consultant or a motivational speaker. Choose whichever field of sales is best for you, and then when you are selling you will be passionate about it from within, and it will help you do a better job because you can feel how much impact you are making while you are selling your offerings to the people in society.

"In sales there are going to be times when you can't make everyone happy. Don't expect to and you won't be disappointed. Just do your best for each client in each situation as it arises. Then, learn from each situation how to do it better the next time." —Tom Hopkins

MY PERSONAL SALES EXPERIENCE

As a salesperson you are going to meet lots of people with lots of questions and negativity about your products or services: some want it for free, some want a discount, and the list goes on and on. The key point is that as a salesperson you want to go from being good to being great.

First and foremost, you must love what you are selling; this will help you learn and master the products inside and out, so if there is any question you can answer it, and demonstrate that you know what you are doing. Treat your customers equally regardless of their age, income, sexual orientation, or their background and above all, try to establish a good relationship with your customers.

The best relationship between you and your customers will last for a long time, and you can get business referrals to their family and friends. Your sales will go up, not just because of good quality, excellent customer service and your business being located in a high foot-traffic area, but also because of how you interact with your customers. People like to feel important, appreciated, and treated with respect and dignity. Treat them like a family member and they will not let you down; they will support you as repeat customers, and then you will build loyal customers, and those are your best customers for your sales.

As a salesperson you must have enough confidence, enthusiasm, and ready smiles, and the ability to respond to people's emotions. When a customer wants to buy something, either they're in need or they just want it with no specific reason, and as a salesperson you have to recognize that so you can respond to their emotion. People are different, so you have to be intuitive about how you approach each and every customer, especially when it comes to conversation: most of the time be conscious of what you're saying, to avoid a misunderstanding which may create a negative environment which is not good for your sales.

For example, you tell a customer, "This product is good for you and it costs $20." If the customer says, "No, it's too expensive," sometimes what they mean is you haven't convinced them well enough that the product is important to them, and also you haven't justified the cost as equal to the value of the product. You have to use all your ability, and the best place to learn how to be a good salesperson is from your customers; see what works better and why. If you cannot answer why they should buy from you then you will have a hard time making lots of sales and eventually you may be fired from your sales job.

> *"You don't close a sale; you open a relationship if you want to build a long-term, successful enterprise." —Patricia Fripp*

You can sell pretty much anything, but the question is what and where? So do the research on your business and your target market. To become the best salesperson, you should build a relationship, as this will create long-term loyal customers. Most of the time people don't just buy products or services, they buy added value, and they love coming back to you because of the relationship you built with them, and this will boost your sales. Keep in mind people can buy products or services almost anywhere and from anyone, but they come to you not only because you are better, but because you are different, and your relationship you built with them will make your customers keep buying from you.

YOUR ABILITY TO COMMUNICATE IS VERY CRUCIAL

> *"A salesman, like the storage battery in your car, is constantly discharging energy. Unless he is recharged at frequent intervals he soon runs dry. This is one of the greatest responsibilities of sales leadership." —R. H. Grant*

In sales, no matter how tired you are or how much explaining you have done to the customers, each customer who comes to you is brand new, and you have to start all over again. That is the key to finding a sales pitch which will engage the customer and convince him or her that what you're selling is what they want, whether it be about color, design, healthy food or durability of goods or, in the case of a house, space, location and a safe environment.

From my personal experience, I was able to win the gold nugget of the150th year anniversary (1852-2002) of Wells Fargo Bank in 2002. I worked hard by being ready most of the time to help any customer who walked in the bank, or if I went out in the field to market the bank's products. I was energetic, excited, fully confident and ready to help anyone who had a question about the bank's products. In general, I was very well-prepared with product knowledge and this gave me lots of confidence and I was ready to meet any challenge from the customers or any competitive bank.

Thus, don't assume things but be specific, so when customers come to you at first when they want to get information about your products or services before they buy, you can show them why it's important to them and why they should buy from you, before you even think about selling to them. When the customer says yes, that's the time you close the sale.

Also, you must love what you sell because when sales are slow only love of what you do will keep you going and it will make you learn the product or service well which will help you be able to demonstrate to the customers and be aware of the different people you are serving. With your communication ability and a full knowledge of your products you will not have any problem, because you may need different sales approaches for different people.

You can learn more from your own customers, just like I learned myself when I was a personal banker selling Wells Fargo Bank products. The best way I learned was by treating each and every customer with respect, and then they were eager to open up to me and that's how I learned from them. In return I tried to serve them based on their different needs and wants without bias of who were the haves and who were the have-nots. You must master salescraft, otherwise it will be hard for you to survive in sales.

PERSONAL EXPERIENCE

![photograph]

150th Anniversary Gold Nugget, winner in 2002.
"When you work hard then you will be rewarded."

CHAPTER TWO

CUSTÖMER
BEHAVIOR

❧ THE EXPECTED LESSONS IN CHAPTER TWO ❧

Why is it so necessary to learn the customer's behavior and their cultural backgrounds?
Buying Power
Information Search
Purchase Decision
Problem Recognition
Evaluation of Their Alternatives
Post-purchase Behavior

How will it help you to understand the buying power of your target customers?

Why is it so important to build a long-lasting relationship with customers?

Why treat everyone equally and with integrity and respect?

"Customers set up a hierarchy of values, wants, and needs based on empirical data, opinions, word-of-mouth references, and previous experiences with products and services. They use that information to make purchasing decisions." —Regis McKenna

BUILDING A LONG-LASTING RELATIONISHIP

Building a long-lasting relationship with customers is the key, so try to communicate clearly and regularly with customers about the value of your products or services. Also try to learn and understand the customer's behavior, how humans think, feel, and act in the marketplace. They may enjoy your products, but the most loyal customers love what you stand for and how you can help them; make it easy for them to see what you're about.

When it comes to converting customers, the secret to more sales is as simple as understanding just what your buyer wants and expects from your business. Therefore, it is important you learn the customer's behavior in the market you want to serve, because the products or services you're trying to sell may be not suitable for the market. No matter how good the products are, or how excellent your service is, if the market is not ready for your offering you will hit a dead end. The best thing to do is either sell what is suitable, or take time to educate people about the benefits of your offering before they buy, like Steve Jobs did with his new invention of a technology product. Sometimes people didn't understand but his sales team took the time to educate the public and eventually most of his products were sold worldwide.

CUSTOMER'S WANTS AND NEEDS

When you are in a sales career the key number one goal is to satisfy your customers, before you even think about closing a sale. So listen to their wants and needs and then show them how your offering can help them, by demonstrating what the benefit is to them. Most of the time the cost is not an issue, it's what the products or services can do for them as customers. That's why you will see suits selling from $200 to up to more than $5000, or a lady's bag from $15 to up to more than $7000; they both do the same basic function but the difference is that some want it for social status and some just to meet their basic need. As a salesperson you have to know all this in order to be on top of your sales game.

"Internalize the Golden Rule of sales that says: All things being equal, people will do business with, and refer business to, those people they know, like and trust." —Bob Burg

CULTURAL BACKGROUND

You can sell pretty much anything from sand to gold, and clothes to food, but to be a top salesperson you have to know the cultural background of the market you are serving. No matter how good the quality of your products or services is, if it is not comparable with the customer's needs and wants, it will be hard to sell to them. Not because you are not good in sales, but because people are not accustomed to what you are offering.

When you learn the customer's background then you can predict their wants and needs and also it can make it easier for you to persuade people to buy your products. When you know how to proceed by having talked to the people in your market, this will build trust between you and them, and very often when they come to buy they will be looking for you, because they feel you respect them just by having taken the time to learn their way of living. I remember doing a case study at San Jose State University in my business school about how to introduce a new product of the MD Company in Latin America. We had to study their way of living then introduce the products and that paved the way to sell the products.

BUYING POWER

People want and need most everything which is good for them, but the question you have to ask yourself as a salesperson is, "What is the buying power of the market you are targeting?" The answer depends on the way in which they earn their income. Some have a very limited income, just enough to buy the basic goods for sustaining life, and some have some disposable income they can afford to spend on extra goods and services. This will help you determine where to put most of your effort in selling and boost your quarterly sales, or if you are selling ideas, see if there is enough support where you are.

You may have to move sometimes to another area where people understand and appreciate your offering and can afford it. For example, in the US, if you are good in technology you most likely would move to the Silicon Valley, California where people are into the tech industry, or if you are good in fashion you may want to go to New York City. These are just a couple of examples, but you can make your own specific analysis based on the market you want or are going to sell your products or services to.

TREAT EVERYONE EQUALLY

Why treat everyone equally and with integrity and respect? The goal is to know your customers and their customs well, so when you are selling to them you can approach them in a way that they feel like you are not just there to get their money, but are a part of their normal of life. Try not to just focus on sales, but also on helping people and building a long-lasting relationship, and this will set you apart from the rest of the salespeople. Once a customer feels comfortable with you, they will also recommend that their family and friends do business with you, and that means more sales for you.

PERSONAL EXPERIENCE

In San Francisco, sales winner trophy 2003.
"We all start at the beginning of the race, but the one who gets to the finish line receives a trophy. It is just a sign of saying thank you for your hard work and an excellent job."

CHAPTER THREE

SHŎPPING
TRENDS

⟨ THE EXPECTED LESSONS IN CHAPTER THREE ⟩

Why be up-to-date with shopping trends?

What are the causes and effects of ups and downs in sales throughout the year?

How can you master sales in traditional, modern and online shopping?

"You have to stay updated on trends, social things and pop culture, you need to stay with the times and keep evolving." —Corey Feldman

BE UP-TO-DATE WITH MARKET TRENDS. CHANGE IN DEMAND

Changes in customers' demands are based on how customers think, feel, and interact with others, and on retail spaces, goods, services, brands, and ideas. Marketing trends are very important to watch if you are in sales. You must be up-to-date with market changes which affect the customer demands and the way people use things. Therefore, as demand changes, sales techniques change from traditional to modern. You always want to be ahead of the game, especially in this global market competition, and if you're lagging behind other people in sales they will take over your market.

SHIFTING OF SALES METHODS

You have to be up-to-date with changes of sales methods in the market, if you want to keep up with high sales and become a master of selling. Sales methods change with the change in the times. You may have to relearn how you used to sell your products or services, and even in politics when you sell your ideas you will not sell the same way five or ten years from now. So you must be constantly learning as you're selling, otherwise new salespeople will come in and take over your customers and all of your sales will shift from high all of the time to the lowest sales. Keep selling and keep learning how to sell, and the best teachers are your customers because if they are happy with you they will keep coming back.

TRADITIONAL SHOPPING

In the old days salespeople were good at going door to door to sell. It was easier to build relationships and trust between salespeople and customers. It was hard to travel from one area to the other, but when well equipped with a knowledge of the products or services it was worthwhile to travel as far as you could because you were going to make money and help people with their needs and wants.

The question to ask is why people buy from you and not from other people who sell almost the same thing as you are selling. The answer is the relationship you build with your customers. People feel comfortable dealing with someone who feels familiar to them. Thus we are constantly selling: either we are selling products, are politicians trying to sell our ideas to the public, or are employees who very often want to hold a certain position in the office based on our talents. The best way to accomplish this is to be a people person; then they will support you.

Most people who did well in the traditional sales of going door to door were very ambitious and enthusiastic about their sales and cared about people, and that's what made them go as far as they could go. So you can use their examples to build on your own strengths and self-determination, whether in a store or in online sales. It is up to you to work hard, stay focused and take action toward your dream. Everything is going to be okay.

MODERN SHOPPING

People will go to a retail store for many reasons, not just to buy. That's why in some stores some customers come in and will not buy until they see so-and-so because they are happy with his/her service; and that tells you when you are in sales pay close attention to serve customers first. If you can remember their name, their favorite sports, dog or anything which makes them feel happy to come see you, it's even better. It will be easier for you to convince them to buy something, and if they say yes then you close the sale.

Since most everything can be seen online and at various stores throughout the town, in your local market and at a mall in the city, the competition is very high. Sometimes people may be selling the same thing as yours, so the best way to handle this is to look around at what is missing in other salespeople's technique.

I learned these techniques at the age of eight in my hometown of Kaliua when I was selling barbeque. I was selling much better than others just by looking at what they were doing wrong and using that as a strong point to defeat them in sales, and I never forgot that method throughout my life in business. Even when I came to America, I was always looking for what was missing in the group that would set me apart and make me the best in sales. Learn what is missing from others and then come up with your own new style; if you do that plus use other people's methods of selling, you will not just become better, but different and unique. This sales pitch mechanism will set you apart from the rest of the group and you will become a master craftsman of selling.

ONLINE SHOPPING

Business started a long time ago, basically since the beginning of mankind. Thus salespeople have been the backbone between producers and consumers. Since nothing stayed the same but constantly changed, sales methods and techniques changed as time went by from traditional to modern and on up to the technological sales aspects of online shopping.

With the change in technology, people started to buy most of their goods and services online. Thus keep in mind that technology makes it easier or harder in sales. In the old days salespeople were good at going door to door to sell, and modern people mostly shop by going to a retail store, but with the change of times, now people order online and have the goods delivered to their house. In the old days, most of the time customers could see you and ask you questions, now as a salesperson sometimes people may not even see you, so your word is your bond. The more they trust you, the more they will come on your site to shop. Keep in mind that people build trust based on promise, and if you don't deliver on your promise in a satisfactory manner or give the customers a good reason why you couldn't deliver on your promise, then next time you may lose a sale.

CAUSES AND EFFECTS OF UPS AND DOWNS IN SALES

There are causes and effects of ups and downs in sales throughout a year. Pay close attention to the seasonal changes from January to December as these changes can affect your sales. As a salesperson you have to keep up with business seasonal sales peak times. This will boost your quarterly sales, and also can give you an idea of what to advise your manager on what to anticipate in upcoming weeks to increase products or services to sell; just be on the lookout for a holiday, festival or any special event.

My sales were always up because I knew at the beginning of school there were new students who needed new accounts and also at a different company new employees needed new accounts. I was looking for any event which could bring more sales; for example, wherever people were in need of a bank product, and when and how to reach them. I stayed very active. Nothing comes easily; be active and creative and you will get lots of sales. Especially if you can predict the seasonal demand of your product, then you are going to sell well. For example, in America:

JANUARY - FEBRUARY - MARCH
The major attraction will be Valentine's and New Year's gifts such as: cars, flowers, clothes, greeting cards, and jewelry.

APRIL - MAY - JUNE
Mother's Day, Father's Day, and traveling time:
jewelry, airline tickets and tools.

JULY - AUGUST - SEPTEMBER
Traveling time, outdoor activities, back to school:
airline tickets, barbecue products, computers, uniforms, books, and clothes.

OCTOBER - NOVEMBER - DECEMBER
Halloween, Thanksgiving, Christmas holidays:
Halloween costumes, food (especially turkey), and gifts of many kinds.

These are just examples in the U.S.A., but it applies to most countries; it may just be in different times and under different names, but the basic fundamental principle is the same. Thus, as a salesperson you have to be ahead of your game in anticipation of different seasons for your products or services so you can let the public know you have what they want and need. By knowing that, you will increase the products and effort at a given time and in return will boost your sales.

❧ PERSONAL EXPERIENCE ❧

Sponsorship Recognition Award

Presented To

TBX Business Consultant

In Recognition and Appreciation
Of
Your Generous Support toward the success
Of the Diaspora Council of Tanzanians in America
(DICOTA) 2012 Convention

Certificate of Sponsorship Recognition presented by the Diaspara Council of Tanzanians in America (DICOTA).
"Try not only to be different, but unique. Knowing and predicting by thinking hard and long will make you excel to the top in your career."

CHAPTER FOUR

PRŎDUCTS

❧ **THE EXPECTED LESSONS IN CHAPTER FOUR** ☙

Why learn well the products you are selling?

What is the importance of learning the demographics of your target market?

Why isn't it about what you sell, but where and how you sell it?

"No matter what your product is, you are ultimately in the education business. Your customers need to be constantly educated about the many advantages of doing business with you, trained to use your products more effectively, and taught how to make never-ending improvement in their lives." —Robert G. Allen

LEARNING YOUR PRODUCTS WELL WILL BUILD CONFIDENCE IN YOU

I f you know something then you talk with confidence. Thus, learn the products you are selling so well that if someone asks about it you can answer without hesitation. The product is something you sell the customer which will give them benefit, so when customers come to you they want you to define and exlain to them what the product will do for them if they buy it. If you have learned well the products you are selling, then you will be able to explain to the customers with confidence and this will build trust between you and the customer about the products you are selling, and he will be very happy to buy from you.

LEARN THE BUYING POWER OF YOUR TARGET MARKET

There are many types of goods and services with different prices. As a salesperson you must learn the buying power of the market you are targeting, so you can sell what they want and they can afford. The simple way to learn the buying power is find out their income, their social status, their cultural norms and their spending habits; these factors will help you to determine whether you will be able to sell well your products or services.

Also you have to learn and understand well your offering so you can demonstrate to the customers with confidence. People very often believe what a salesperson tells them and if you can show the customers you know what you are selling then people have no problem buying from you, and your sales will go up more than the other people in your sales group.

Your ability to define and explain in depth about your offering will not only create confidence in you for the customer, but also will increase your sales. So take time to learn and relearn until you become the master of your endeavor and when you go into the sales field you go boldly and full of confidence, ready to face and answer any unexpected and expected questions regarding the products or services you are selling. Since you are aware of their buying power and you have full knowledge of what you are offering them, then the only thing you need to explain to them with your communication skills is why they should buy, and you will do well in sales.

IT IS NOT WHAT YOU SELL, IT IS WHERE AND HOW THAT IS YOUR SALES TECHNIQUE

Defining and explaining is very important when you are in sales, whatever you are selling. To know if you have a good understanding of what you are selling the test is very simple: if someone asks what you sell you can tell them without reading a paper or giving them a "maybe" answer. You have to know it from the bottom of your heart. You can read just to remind yourself but the best practice is if everything is on top of your head. In my case, when I worked at the bank I knew all the products I was selling by heart and it was not easy, but it made me win the gold medal for being one of the top 2% best salespeople nationwide in the U.S. in 2003.

✥ PERSONAL EXPERIENCE ✥

![Photo]

The top 2% medal national wide Wells Fargo Bank. Winner 2003.
"If you love and learn your product or service that you are dealing with, you will sell well with confidence and be rewarded for your professionalism."

CHAPTER FIVE

SERVICES

❦ THE EXPECTED LESSONS IN CHAPTER FIVE ❧

Why are the best practices of selling services: support, satisfaction, marketing, information, loyalty, value, care, offer, experience, relationship, help, and focused?

What is the difference between selling products and services?

If selling services is selling something invisible, as people are buying a promise, then what does it take for them to trust you?

The customer's view of your character is formed by the image you present.

"The best prospect is the client who has already dealt with you. The second best is the one referred to you by a client who has dealt with you previously. The third best is the one referred to you by another trusted professional or friend." —Marilyn Jennings.

THE DIFFERENCE BETWEEN SELLING PRODUCTS AND SERVICES

S elling services is selling invisible things; people cannot touch or feel but they can have faith, trust and confidence in what you are telling them about how it is going to work and solve their problems. Thus it requires your credibility, sincerity and knowledge of the materials you are telling people are going to work. Thus, at first it is hard because people have no history with you, but don't let that discourage you. Keep selling your ideas and eventually you are going to be a master.

SELLING SERVICES IS SELLING A PROMISE

"Understand that you need to sell you and your ideas in order to advance your career, gain more respect, and increase your success, influence and income." —Jay Abraham

Selling services is different than selling products: people can touch, feel, or smell the product, but with services what they buy is a promise which they believe from you. Thus, it is very hard to sell to a stranger who doesn't know you well; that is why you have to market yourself as a credible person, then people will build trust around you and then they will be willing to do business with you.

There is a saying, "Seeing is believing." When you touch you can feel and when you smell you can identify, but in service there is mostly none of the above, except they have to see the way you behave in order to believe you, so you become a product. Therefore, try to watch your actions and be guided by moral virtue, and then people will either do business with you or they will recommend you to someone for your services.

For example, I'd like to give special thanks to many of my customers who recommended me to their friends and family over the years in my sales career, from my own business to Wells Fargo, and these made it possible for me to win lots of awards and stay in my own business for over 30 years, due to the good sales I received from my loyal customers who trusted me. The main reasons behind my sales success is I treated all my customers like family or best friends, to name a few.

One of the recommendations was from Mr. Edward J. and Mrs. Emma F. Welsh of Sunnyvale, CA at Wells Fargo bank:

SUNNYVALE, CA 94089-1745

MAY 9, 2002

REENA S. CARVALLO, V.P/BRANCH MGR.

WELLS FARGO BANK, N.A

590 CASTRO STREET

MOUNTAIN VIEW, CA 94041

RE: YASSINI KAPUYA (#C8163)

DEAR MS. CARVALLO,

TODAY AT YOUR BRANCH WE WERE ASSISTED BY MR. KAPUYA. HE RECTIFIED AND

SIMPLIFIED SEVERAL MATTERS FOR US.

"YASSINI" WAS PROFESSIONAL, COURTEOUS, AND CONGENIAL.

WHAT DOES A CUSTOMER (OR CLIENT) LOOK FOR IN A BANKER?

"A PERSON YOU CAN TRUST."

SINCERELY,

EDWARD J. WELSH AND EMMA F. WELSH

Your sincerity will build credibility and those are your tools which will serve you as a mirror to reflect to people who you are and what you are trying to serve. If they see you're a credible person most people will be willing to do business with you, and that will be your base to build up your sales. People look for your ability and willingness to help. Whatever service you have decided to pursue, you will do well if you chose sales to be your career, especially if you are following your passion. The key is to be specific about what kind of service you want to provide; this is best because you cannot know everything. Thus, find the service you like, learn it inside and out and then sell it to the public, then you will be on your way to success.

THE CUSTOMER'S VIEW OF YOUR CHARACTER IS FORMED BY THE IMAGE YOU PRESENT

In the service business, your credibility is essential. If you are selling services you must be credible; in other words, you must deliver what you promise in a timely manner, show what you have done, have people testify about your service, try to look professional most of the time (you never know where and when you are going to meet new clients) and last, carry your business card all the time. These things will draw many people's attention to the fact that you are credible enough to do business with and that you will not waste their time or money based on false promises.

Keep in mind that in the service business your goal is: to help, assist, guide, support and advise people, which will lead them in the right direction. Thus, be very honest and sincere with what you are telling people, otherwise it will reflect badly on you, because most of the time bad information travels faster than good.

To avoid making unnecessary mistakes, if you cannot do the job let the client know you cannot, or ask them to give you more time to do more research rather than just agree because you want the money. One bad apple can spoil all the others, and in your case once your credibility is in question then that is most likely the beginning of your downfall in selling business services. There is no magic in selling an invisible, you can do it as long as you have enough knowledge of the service you are offering, watch your tongue, look professional, deliver what you promise on time, and most importantly, be yourself, then you will be on your way to the top sales guru's club.

PERSONAL EXPERIENCE

Certificate of appreciation presented by Ali Hassani, former President of Tanzania. "When you treat people equally with respect and integrity, then you will receive back not only their business but also appreciation and respect among your peers."

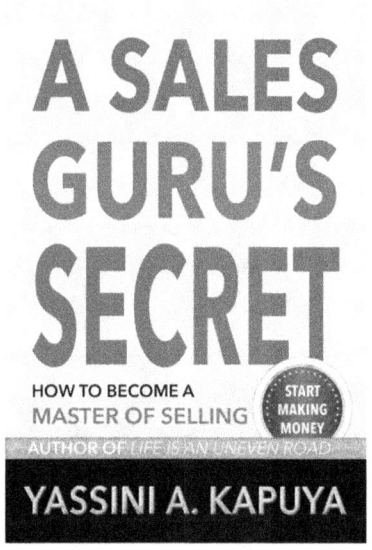

Above all, you must know well your customers, shopping trends, and what you're offering well enough that even when you are asked about them in the middle of the night you can answer without hesitation. To be an excellent salesperson, most of the time it's not about what you are selling, but about you as a person and how you sell. This starts with your communication skills, good ethical behavior, knowledge of the products or services, and credibility. These qualities will show if you are trustworthy enough to do business with.

Also, your ability to predict customers' wants and needs based on learning and watching market changes due to seasonal, technological and demographic changes (because every so often people move in and out and they bring new tastes and styles of living), will help you better your position in sales above all your colleagues. Just remember that what you sold and how you sold it today may not be the same five or ten years from now, thus you have to be constantly relearning.

That's why very often, even at university level, you will see most academic people go for a sabbatical now and then just to re-polish their understanding and keep up with changes. In the same way, many career people attend meetings to learn new skills and new offerings in the market, since that is a law of nature: nothing stays same but constant change. I wish you all the best. Go sell!

YOU WERE BORN TO SELL. WHAT AND HOW YOU WILL NOT KNOW UNTIL YOU TRY.

ABOUT THE AUTHOR

Yassini A. Kapuya was born in Tanzania. He is a senior business consultant and founder of TBX Business Consulting Co. and Co-Founder of Tanzanian Chamber of commerce in America. He worked at Wells Fargo Bank as a Senior Membership Consultant and as an office manager at H&R Block Income Tax Preparation Company in Menlo Park. He wrote this book based on his business experience and work ethics of over 20 years and the inspiration he got from his customers. In 2005, he earned his BS degree in marketing and sales from San Jose State University in California. In 2000, he received an Associate Degree in business administration from Foothill College in California. He also received his certificate in Internal Revenue Service (IRS) from Fresno, California in 2000. In 1996, he received a certificate in business planning and management from a start up micro business initiative in Menlo Park, CA. He was the winner of the 150 years Gold Nugget Anniversary of Wells Fargo Bank for sales in 2002. He was also the winner of the top 2% in sales for Wells Fargo Bank in the U.S. in 2003.

Mr. Kapuya is the author of *The 7 Lessons to Succeed in Business* and *Life Is an Uneven Road. A Sales's Guru Secret* completes the series for personal growth and prosperity in business.

www.ingramcontent.com/pod-product-compliance
Lightning Source LLC
Chambersburg PA
CBHW071002180526
45168CB00003B/1249